I'M **ALLERGIC** TO...
Nuts

Written by E.C. Andrews

Published in 2025 by
KidHaven Publishing, an Imprint of
Greenhaven Publishing, LLC
2544 Clinton St., Buffalo, NY 14224

© 2024 BookLife Publishing Ltd.

Written by: E.C. Andrews
Edited by: Rebecca Phillips-Bartlett
Designed by: Jasmine Pointer

All facts, statistics, web addresses and URLs in this book were verified as valid and accurate at time of writing. No responsibility for any changes to external websites or references can be accepted by either the author or publisher.

Cataloging-in-Publication Data

Names: Andrews, E.C.
Title: Nuts / E.C. Andrews.
Description: Buffalo, NY : KidHaven Publishing, 2025. | Series: I'm allergic to… | Includes glossary and index.
Identifiers: ISBN 9781534549074 (pbk.) | ISBN 9781534549081 (library bound) | ISBN 9781534549098 (ebook)
Subjects: LCSH: Food allergy in children--Juvenile literature. | Nuts--Juvenile literature. | Peanuts--Juvenile literature. | Food allergy--Juvenile literature.
Classification: LCC RJ386.5 A53 2025 | DDC 616.97'5--dc23

All rights reserved.

No part of this book may be reproduced in any form without permission in writing from the publisher, except by a reviewer.

Manufactured in the United States of America

CPSIA compliance information: Batch #CW25KH
For further information contact Greenhaven Publishing LLC at 1-844-317-7404.

Please visit our website,
www.greenhavenpublishing.com.
For a free color catalog of all our high-quality books, call toll free 1-844-317-7404
or fax 1-844-317-7405.

Find us on

Image Credits

All images are courtesy of Shutterstock.com. With thanks to Getty Images, Thinkstock Photo and iStockphoto.
Cover – Meranda19, Anatoliy Karlyuk, Roman Samokhin, Evikka, oksana2010, Hurst Photo, Nitr, Rtstudio, Jiri Hera. Throughout – Meranda19. 4–5 – marilyn barbone, Kaspars Grinvalds. 6–7 – Pixel-Shot, Dionisvera. 8–9 – Pavel Rumme, Cryptsie, Marys Poly. 10–11 – bigacis, Nataliia Pyzhova, Pixel-Shot, Diana Vucane. 12–13 – Pixel-Shot, Keith Homan. 14–15 – Richard M Lee, ZAHRA22, Anwarul Kabir Photo. 16–17 – Tatevosian Yana, Lotus Images, Maks Narodenko, Enlightened Media, Tim UR, RGB_art. 18–19 – Picture Partners, adison pangchai, Olga Miltsova, Wiktory, kopava, Anatolir. 20–21 – amphaiwan, bergamont. 22–23 – Hananeko_Studio, Rawpixel.com.

Contents

Page 4	Delicious Diets
Page 6	What Is an Allergy?
Page 8	What Are Nuts?
Page 10	What Are Nut Products?
Page 12	Symptoms of a Nut Allergy
Page 14	Smart Swaps
Page 16	Fantastic Fiber
Page 18	Nut-Free Pesto Sauce
Page 20	Nut-Free Florentines
Page 22	Allergies and Us
Page 24	Glossary and Index

Words that look like **THIS** can be found in the glossary on page 24.

Delicious Diets

Our diet is made up of all the different foods we eat. Eating different types of food is called a balanced diet. Eating a balanced diet is important for keeping our minds and bodies healthy.

Some people cannot eat certain foods. This could be because of an allergy. Allergies might make eating a balanced diet feel more challenging. However, there are plenty of yummy foods you can safely enjoy.

What Is an Allergy?

An allergy is when your body has a bad **REACTION** to something that is usually harmless. This is because your body mistakes it for something dangerous. Some allergic reactions are more serious than others.

Allergic reactions can make you feel very sick. There are many different allergies. There are some allergies that not many people have. Other allergies are more common. Being allergic to nuts is very common.

What Are Nuts?

Tree nuts are hard-shelled fruits that grow on trees. Tree nuts include almonds, Brazil nuts, pecans, hazelnuts, and walnuts.

Tree nuts

Peanuts are not actually a type of nut. Peanuts are a type of **LEGUME**.

Peanuts

Peanuts and tree nuts are two different allergies. They are both very common. Many people with a tree nut allergy may also have a peanut allergy. These two allergies can have similar **SYMPTOMS**.

What Are Nut Products?

Nuts and peanuts can be eaten whole as snacks. They are also used as **INGREDIENTS** in other foods. Different kinds of nuts can be found in foods such as chocolate, ice cream, and breakfast cereals.

Cereal

Nuts are often used in desserts, such as chocolate and ice cream.

Chocolate

Ice cream

Nuts in foods cannot always be seen. If you have a nut allergy, it is important to read the labels when trying new foods. Avoid foods with labels that say:

- Contains nuts
- May contain nuts
- Made in a factory that also handles nuts

Nuts can also be found in some shampoos and skin lotions.

Symptoms of a Nut Allergy

If you feel unwell after eating nuts, go straight to a grown-up. A nut allergy can make people feel symptoms such as:

- Itchy or **SWELLING** skin
- Runny nose
- A tight feeling in your throat
- Trouble breathing
- Stomach pain
- Feeling or being sick

Anaphylaxis is a very serious allergic reaction. If you have a serious nut allergy, always keep your autoinjector with you if you have one. An autoinjector **INJECTS** medicine into your body that can help with anaphylaxis.

Autoinjector

Smart Swaps

Pumpkin seeds can also make a yummy snack.

Nuts are often used in cooking to add **FLAVOR**. You can do the same with different kinds of seeds and vegetables. Pumpkin seeds can be used to make delicious nut-free pasta sauces.

Chickpeas can have a nutty flavor. They are soft when boiled and crunchy when roasted. If you are making something sweet, puffed rice can add some nut-free crunch to your baking.

Roasted chickpeas

Puffed rice

Fantastic Fiber

Fiber is an important part of a balanced diet. Eating fiber helps keep your stomach healthy. Nuts contain lots of fiber. However, fiber can be found in other foods too.

Nut-Free Pesto Sauce

To make some fantastic nut-free pesto sauce, you will need:

- 2 peeled garlic cloves
- 1 cup of fresh basil leaves (or more if you like!)
- 1/4 cup of pumpkin seeds
- 1/4 cup of grated parmesan cheese
- 2/3 cup of olive oil

Garlic cloves

Pumpkin seeds

Basil leaves

Let's cook!

- Preheat your oven to 400 degrees Fahrenheit (200 degrees Celsius).
- Pour a little bit of olive oil onto your garlic.
- Roast your garlic in the oven for 15 minutes.
- Add the pumpkin seeds to your garlic and roast for 5 more minutes.
- With a bit more olive oil, use a blender to grind up the garlic, the pumpkin seeds, and the basil leaves.
- Stir in your grated parmesan cheese.
- Enjoy!

Nut-Free Florentines

Florentines are a classic cookie usually made with nuts – but not these Florentines! You will need:

- 1 cup of nut-free cornflakes
- 4 dried apricots
- 1/4 cup of dried currants
- 1/4 cup of raisins
- 1/2 cup of dried coconut
- 1 1/4 tablespoons of flour
- 1/4 cup of heavy cream
- 1/3 cup of sugar
- 2 tablespoons of honey
- 4 ounces of melted dark chocolate

Apricots

Currants

Let's cook!

- Preheat your oven to 350 degrees Fahrenheit (180 degrees Celsius).
- Chop your dried fruits. Mix them with your cornflakes, flour, and coconut.
- Make caramel by melting the cream, sugar, and honey until it becomes **LIQUID**.
- Mix your caramel with your dried fruit mix.
- Put small blobs of the mixture onto a baking tray.
- Bake for 7 minutes until golden.
- When cool, dip your Florentines into your melted dark chocolate.

Allergies and Us

It is normal to feel a bit worried if you find out you have a nut allergy. However, there are still many tasty foods you can safely enjoy as part of a balanced diet.

Which recipe are you excited to try?

If you are trying a new food, always check whether it has nuts in it. Ask a grown-up if you are not sure. There are lots of nut-free **RECIPES** waiting to be explored!

Glossary

flavor — how something tastes

ingredients — food items that are combined with other foods to make a particular dish

injects — pushes a liquid into something using a needlelike object

legume — a plant that produces seeds in pods

liquid — a material that flows, such as water

reaction — something done or felt in response to something else

recipes — instructions explaining how to make certain foods or dishes

swelling — becoming bigger than normal

symptoms — signs of an illness that can be used to tell what is wrong with someone

Index

allergies 5–7, 9, 11–13, 22
chocolate 10, 20–21
diets 4–5, 16, 22
fiber 16–17
food 4–5, 10–11, 16, 22–23
fruit 8, 17, 21
peanuts 8–10
seeds 14, 18–19
vegetables 14, 17